Contents

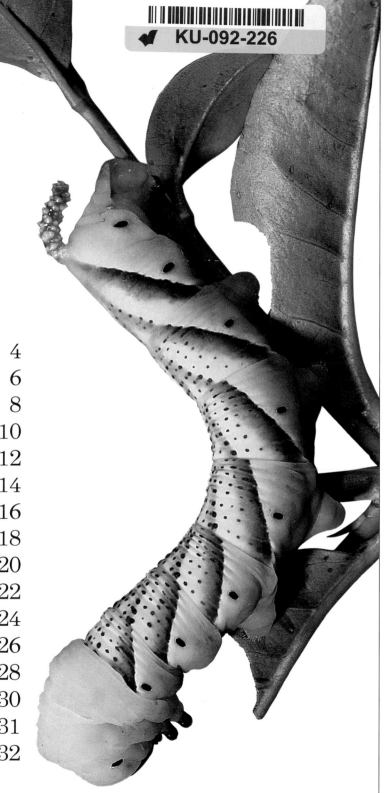

The publishers wish to thank the following for permission to reproduce copyright material:

Oxford Scientific Films and individual copyright holders on the following pages: G I Bernard 5 bottom, 10 left, 11 top left, 21 right; Mike Birkhead title page; Neil Bromhall 11 bottom left; George K Bryce/Animals Animals 14 top; J A L Cooke 10 bottom, 14/15; John Cooke 15 top; Michael Fogden 16/17, 27 left; D G Fox contents page, 4 bottom; Harry Fox 26; Bob Fredrick 9 top; Breck P Kent/Animals Animals 22/23; London Scientific Films 19 bottom; Alastair MacEwan 19 top; G A Maclean 5 top; Colin Milkins 12; Patti Murray/Animals Animals 18, 20/21; Stan Osolinski 21 left; Oxford Scientific Films 23 top; Helen W Price 22 top; Avril Ramage 10 top; Kjell Sandved cover, 20 bottom; Dr Friedrich Sauer/Okapia 27 top; David Shale 11 right; D R Specker/Animals Animals 16 left; Sinclair Stammers 28/29; Harold Taylor 17 top; K G Vock/Okapia 4 top; P & W Ward 27 bottom.

First published in the UK in 2003 by
Chrysalis Children's Books
An imprint of Chrysalis Books Group Plc
The Chrysalis Building, Bramley Road,
London W10 6SP

Paperback edition first published in 2005

Printed in China

ISBN 1 84138 630 8 (hb)
ISBN 1 84458 383 X (pb)

British Library Cataloguing in Publication Data
CIP data for this book is available from the British Library

Editor: Veronica Ross
Designers: Frances McKay and James Lawrence
Consultant: Steve Pollock

Words in **bold** are in the glossary on page 30.

Title page picture:
A tiger moth feeding on a flower.

Contents page picture:
This caterpillar will change into a death's-head hawk moth.

◄ This insect is a blowfly. You probably see more flies than any other kind of insect.

▲ The wings of this peacock butterfly have many colours and a beautiful pattern.

► A thrip is a tiny insect that lives in plants. It has two narrow wings which are folded over its back.

Adult insects have six legs. Spiders have eight legs so they are not insects. Most insects have two pairs of wings, but some insects have only one pair. Many young insects have no wings.

On the outside

An insect's body is nothing like ours. Most of its head is taken up by two huge eyes. It also has three small eyes and two long antennae or feelers.

The middle part of the body is the **thorax**. The wings and six legs are attached to the thorax. The back part of an insect is called the **abdomen**.

▶ An insect's body is made up of three parts – the head, thorax and abdomen.

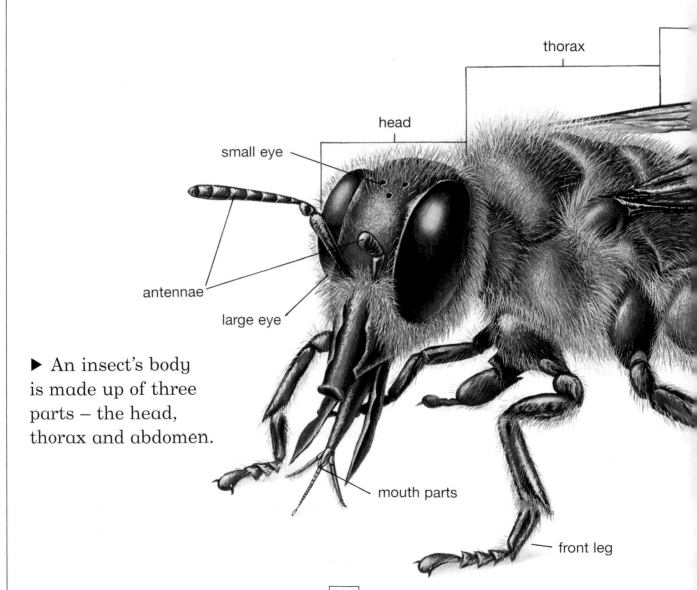

thorax

head

small eye

antennae

large eye

mouth parts

front leg

Insects have no bones inside their bodies. Instead they are covered with a hard skin, like a suit of armour, which protects their insides.

▲ You cannot see the three parts of a shield bug's body because they are covered by its wings.

An insect's hard outer skin is made of **chitin**. It does not stretch as the insect grows. An insect sheds its outer skin when it becomes too small and grows a new one.

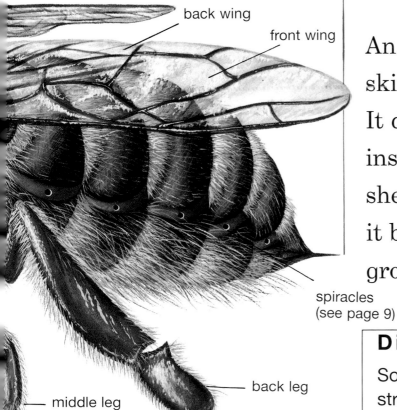

abdomen

back wing

front wing

spiracles (see page 9)

middle leg

back leg

Did you know?

Some beetles have amazingly strong jaws. Their jaws are so strong they can bite through the metals copper and zinc.

On the inside

Insects have to breathe and eat like all other animals. Special organs inside their bodies process air and food. Air is taken in through breathing holes along the side of the body.

Food passes from the mouth to the **gizzard** and stomach where it is slowly broken down. An insect's heart is a long tube. It pumps blood to all parts of the insect's body.

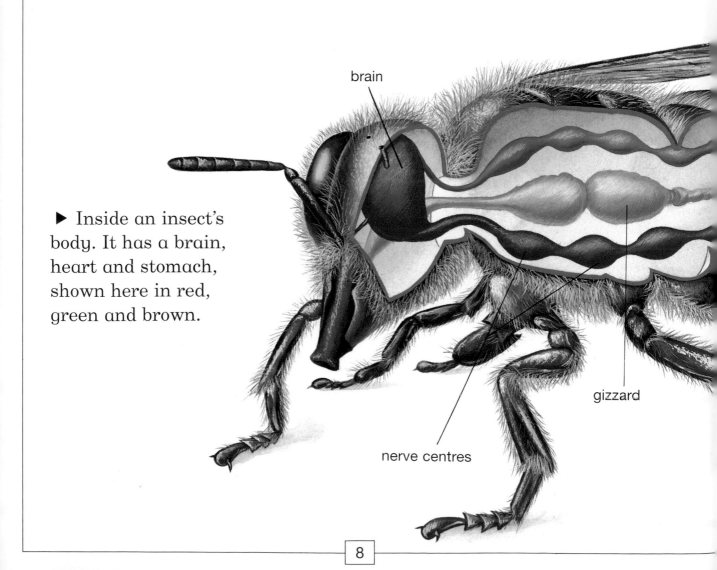

▶ Inside an insect's body. It has a brain, heart and stomach, shown here in red, green and brown.

brain

gizzard

nerve centres

8

An insect cannot think because its brain is very simple. Nerve centres in the body make different parts of the body work. Flying and walking are controlled by nerve centres in the thorax.

▲ The black spots on the side of this caterpillar are **spiracles**, or breathing holes.

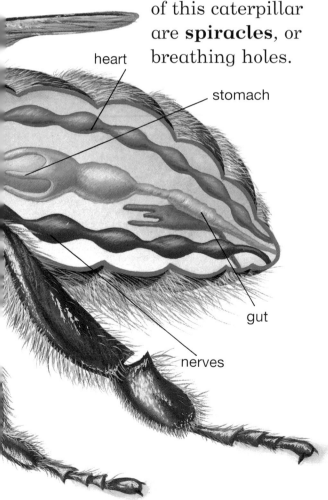

heart

stomach

gut

nerves

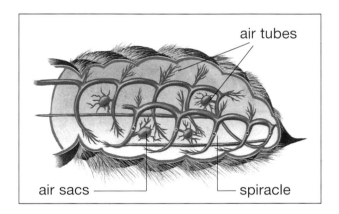

air tubes

air sacs

spiracle

▲ An insect takes in air through its spiracles. The air passes into a network of tubes and **air sacs**.

Did you know?

An insect's blood is not carried around its body through tubes like our veins and arteries. Instead the blood just swirls around inside the insect's body.

Changes

Most insects go through four stages to become an adult. They begin life as a tiny egg which **hatches** into a **larva**.

▲ You cannot tell from looking at them that these black and yellow caterpillars will turn into moths with red spots and stripes.

A larva is a young insect. More than one larva are called larvae. Most larvae look very different from the adults they turn into.

The life cycle of a ladybird

1 A ladybird has laid these yellow eggs on a nettle leaf. Ladybird larvae will hatch from the eggs.

4 The pupa splits open and the adult ladybird crawls out. The ladybird eats greenfly and looks for a good place to lay its eggs.

The larva eats and grows. Some larvae have legs and move around to find food. Others have no legs and feed where they are.

2 The ladybird larva only eats other animals. Here it is eating a greenfly.

▲ Hornets, bees and wasps all lay their eggs in a nest. The adults look after and feed the larvae.

3 When the larva has grown big enough, it turns into a pupa. Inside this tough, outer skin, the larva changes into an adult ladybird.

When it is fully grown, the larva becomes a **pupa** and changes into an adult. This change is called **metamorphosis**.

Nymphs and naiads

Some insects go through three stages to become an adult. The egg hatches into a **nymph** which looks much like a small, wingless adult. Mayfly, earwigs and grasshoppers all develop from nymphs.

Some nymphs, such as those of dragonflies, spend all their time in water. They are called **naiads**. The adults have wings and live on land.

▼ The young mayfly nymph lives under water in a stream.

▲ Only adult insects have wings. The wings of this desert locust began as wing buds on the nymph (see below).

The nymph of a desert locust.

Laying eggs

▼ A fly's eggs hatch into maggots.

The female lays her eggs where there is food for the young. Many caterpillars that hatch from moth and butterfly eggs eat only one kind of leaf. So moths and butterflies must lay their eggs on the right kind of plant. Flies often lay their eggs on rotting meat. The **maggots** feed on the meat when they hatch.

Some insects grow so big they burst out of their eggs. Others have sharp spines which they use to cut through the eggshell.

▶ This shield bug guards her eggs until they hatch. Some of the eggs have already hatched.

► A caterpillar
hatches.

Feet and legs

Insects use their feet for gripping. Some insects have claws at the end of their legs to help them grip. Flies have sticky pads that allow them to walk upside-down across ceilings.

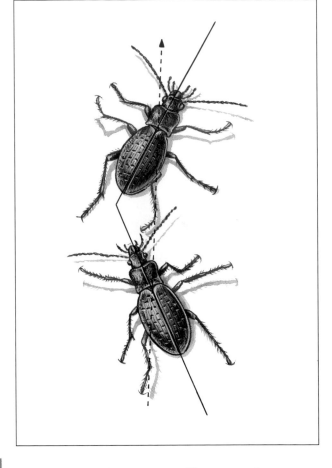

▲ How an insect walks on six legs. The legs shown in red are off the ground at the same time.

◄ This beetle has claws to grip a rough surface.

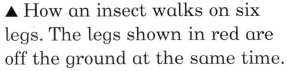

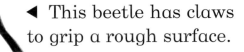

Insects with long legs can usually run very fast. Each leg is covered with hard chitin and can bend at the body, the knee and the ankle.

Grasshoppers and locusts have very long back legs. They can jump up to ten times the length of their bodies.

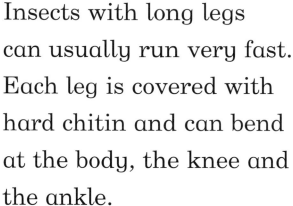

▲ This grasshopper jumps by pushing itself up on its long back legs.

▼ A caterpillar holds on with its legs and moves by stretching its body a bit at a time.

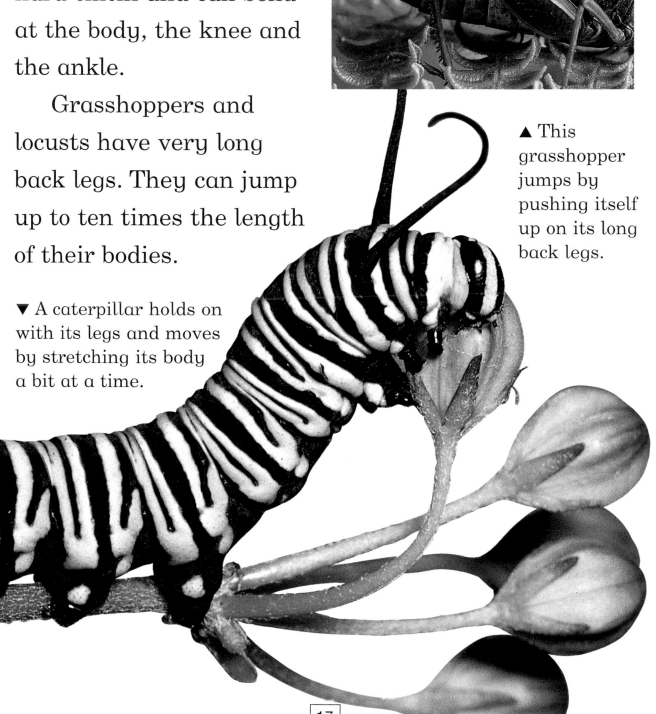

Flying

Most kinds of insect can fly. Some have one pair of wings, others have two pairs. They are made of two very thin sheets of chitin. The wings of butterflies and moths are covered in thousands of tiny scales.

▲ Monarch butterflies fly long distances from Canada to Mexico. Here, they stop for a drink.

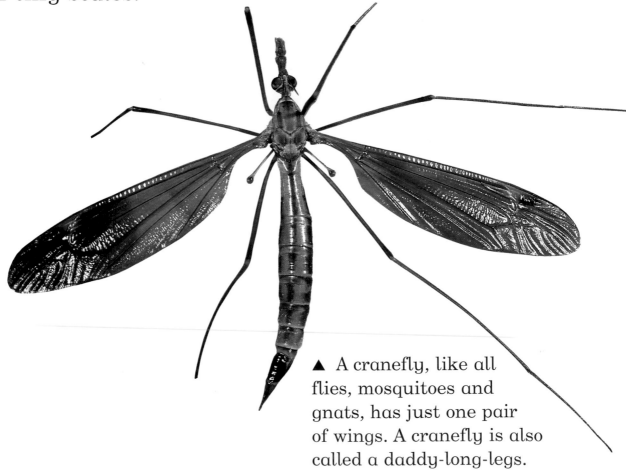

▲ A cranefly, like all flies, mosquitoes and gnats, has just one pair of wings. A cranefly is also called a daddy-long-legs.

▲ You can only see a ladybird's wings when it is flying. At other times, the horny front wings cover and protect the back wings.

To fly, an insect beats its wings up and down very fast. This pushes it up and forwards. Hoverflies can fly sideways, backwards, and hover in one place. Some butterflies and horseflies can fly very fast, up to 50 kilometres an hour.

▶ Bees, like many other insects, have two pairs of wings. Tiny hooks join the two pairs of wings together.

Seeing and hearing

An insect sees the world quite differently from us. Its huge eyes are made up of thousands of tiny eyes. Each tiny eye sees a slightly different picture.

▼ A horsefly's huge eyes stick out from its head so it can see all around.

▲ A dragonfly can see so well, it can catch mosquitoes in the half dark.

Most insects can hear, but they do not have ears as we do. Instead they pick up sounds through the hairs on their bodies. Some insects have **eardrums** on their bodies.

Insects do not have a voice, like we do. Bees hum because their wings beat so fast. Crickets make a clicking sound by rubbing their wings together.

◀ A grasshopper sings by rubbing its back legs together. Its eardrum is just under its wing, and is shown close up below.

Tasting and smelling

All insects have two feelers called antennae on their heads. They use them to feel, to smell and to taste. The silk moth can smell so well with his antennae, he can detect a female many kilometres away.

Insects also taste with the hairs on their body. Some butterflies can taste more with the hairs on their legs than we do with our tongues.

▲ A silk moth has big, feathery antennae.

Did you know?

A fly can taste a drop of sugar with the tip of one hair on the end of its leg.

▲ Ants recognize each other by touching their antennae together.

◀ This beetle uses its long antennae to taste and smell.

What do insects eat?

A grasshopper has strong, sharp jaws. It uses them to cut off pieces of plant.

The shape of an insect's mouth depends on the kind of food it eats. Most insects feed on plants – on leaves, flowers, stems or roots. Caterpillars munch leaves. Bees and many other insects help plants. They spread **pollen** as they drink the sweet juice called **nectar** from inside the flowers.

◄ A fly's mouth has a soft pad at the end. It spits on its food to soften it and then sucks it up.

◄ A mosquito's mouth is a long, hollow needle with a sharp point. It jabs the skin of another animal and then sucks up its blood.

Some insects harm plants. A swarm of locusts can destroy all the plants in an area. Many insects eat wood. Termites can destroy whole houses made of wood.

Some insects eat other insects, and some suck the blood of animals. Other insects feed on dung, and others on dead plants and animals. They help to keep the world clean and healthy.

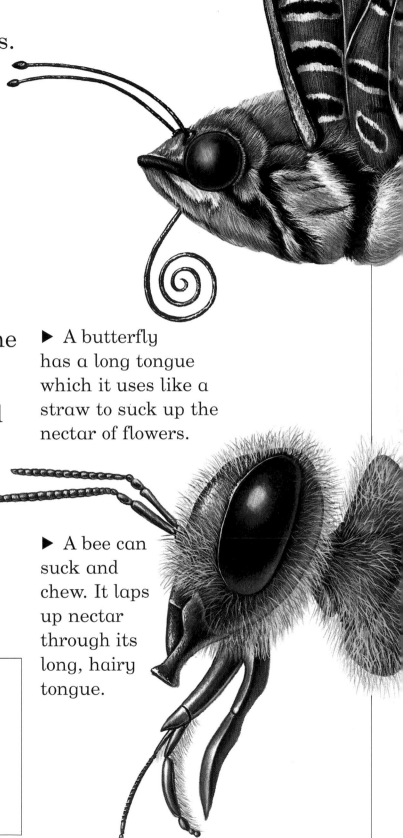

▶ A butterfly has a long tongue which it uses like a straw to suck up the nectar of flowers.

▶ A bee can suck and chew. It laps up nectar through its long, hairy tongue.

Did you know?

Some insects eat strange things. Earwigs nibble bars of soap and household scraps. Cockroaches chew old boots.

World of insects

▶ There are a huge number of different kinds of beetle. This is a stag beetle.

No one knows how many kinds of insect there are. More than a million kinds have been found so far. There are probably more kinds of insects than all other kinds of animals put together.

Insects live almost everywhere, in deserts, forests and the soil. Some even live in the icy Arctic. They live on the warm bodies of animals. Many larvae live in fresh water, and a few live in the sea.

Glossary

Abdomen The large back part of an insect's body. Inside are the stomach, guts and organs for laying eggs.

Air sac Tiny pockets full of air at the end of the air tubes.

Antennae The two feelers on an insect's head. Insects use them to feel, smell and taste.

Chitin The tough substance that covers an insect's body. Its wings are made of thin layers of chitin.

Eardrum A thin sheet of skin which detects sound.

Gizzard An extra stomach which helps to break up food. Insects have no teeth, so the muscles in the gizzard break up food before it passes into the stomach.

Hatch To break out of an egg.

Larva A young insect after it has hatched out of the egg.

Maggot The larva of a fly. A maggot has no legs and has to feed where it hatches.

Metamorphosis The change an insect goes through from an egg to an adult.

Naiads Nymphs which live all the time in water.

Nectar The sugary juice inside some flowers.

Nymph A young insect which looks much like the adult. Nymphs do not form pupae as larvae do, but simply grow larger and develop wings.

Organ A part of the body with a particular job to do, such as the heart, stomach, eyes and brain.

Pollen A fine dust in flowers that helps seeds to grow.

Pupa An insect in the process of changing from a larva to an adult.

Spiracles Holes along the sides of an insect's body which lead to breathing tubes inside its body.

Thorax The middle part of an insect's body.

Key facts

Largest flying insect The Goliath beetle can grow up to 15 cm long, and weigh 100 grams. Longhorn beetles and Rhinoceros beetles are very big too.

Longest insect A kind of stick insect that grows up to 30 cm long.

Smallest insect Feather-winged beetles are less than 0.25 mm long, smaller than this full-stop.

Largest insect ever Giant dragonflies lived 300 million years ago. Their wings were up to 75 cm across, as wide as the wings of a large bird. They lived at the same time as some of the dinosaurs.

Earliest known insects Fossils have been found of insects which lived 390 million years ago. They had no wings and looked very much like today's silverfish.

Most legs The name millipede means 'a thousand feet', but most millipedes have less than 700 legs.

Largest group of insects There are more than 250,000 different kinds of beetles, the largest group of insects.

Largest nest Bees, wasps and ants are just some of the insects that build nests. The largest nests are built by termites. A large nest may tower 10 metres above the ground and have underground chambers reaching 10 metres below ground.

Highest jumper Fleas are tiny, but they can jump 20 cm high – 130 times their own height. If humans could jump as well as a flea, they could jump over a skyscraper.

Most valuable cocoon Some larvae spin a cocoon to protect the pupae. The silkworm moth spins its cocoon of silk thread. On silk farms the cocoon is unravelled and the silk is made into cloth.

Most moults As an insect grows, its hard, outer covering does not grow too. Instead an insect sheds its skin, or moults, as it grows. Dragonflies moult up to 15 times.

Index